DATE DUE			

201298

796.962
PET

Peters, Chris
(Writer)

Great moments in
Olympic ice hockey

HUDSON BEND MIDDLE SCHOOL

INSIDE THE WORLD OF SPORTS

ICE HOCKEY

INSIDE THE WORLD OF SPORTS

AUTO RACING

BASEBALL

BASKETBALL

EXTREME SPORTS

FOOTBALL

GOLF

GYMNASTICS

ICE HOCKEY

LACROSSE

SOCCER

TENNIS

TRACK & FIELD

WRESTLING

INSIDE THE WORLD OF SPORTS

ICE HOCKEY

by Andrew Luke

MASON CREST

Mason Crest
450 Parkway Drive, Suite D
Broomall, Pennsylvania 19008
(866) MCP-BOOK (toll free)

First printing
9 8 7 6 5 4 3 2 1

Names: Luke, Andrew, author.
Title: Ice hockey / Andrew Luke.
Description: Broomall, Pennsylvania : Mason Crest, [2017] | Series: Inside
  the world of sports | Includes index.
Identifiers: LCCN 2015046236 (print) | LCCN 2016015609 (ebook) | ISBN
  9781422234631 (hardback) | ISBN 9781422234556 (series) | ISBN
  9781422284254 (ebook) | ISBN 9781422284254 (eBook)
Subjects: LCSH: Hockey--History.
Classification: LCC GV846.5 .L85 2017 (print) | LCC GV846.5 (ebook) | DDC
  796.962--dc23
LC record available at https://lccn.loc.gov/2015046236

QR CODES AND LINKS TO THIRD-PARTY CONTENT

CONTENTS

KEY ICONS TO LOOK FOR:

Words to understand: These words with their easy-to-understand definitions will increase the reader's understanding of the text while building vocabulary skills.

Educational Videos: Readers can view videos by scanning our QR codes, providing them with additional educational content to supplement the text. Examples include news coverage, moments in history, speeches, iconic sports moments and much more!

Text-dependent questions: These questions send the reader back to the text for more careful attention to the evidence presented there.

Research projects: Readers are pointed toward areas of further inquiry connected to each chapter. Suggestions are provided for projects that encourage deeper research and analysis.

The Stanley Cup is the oldest professional sports trophy in North America. Its namesake, Lord Frederick Stanley of Preston, originally donated it while he was governor general of Canada in 1892. The Cup has been the championship trophy of the National Hockey League since 1926. Every player to win the Cup has his name inscribed on it. The original 7.2" x 11.4" (18.3 x 30.0 cm) Cup sits atop today's modern 35" (88.9 cm) high trophy, which was designed in 1958 and weighs 35 lbs. (15.9 kg).

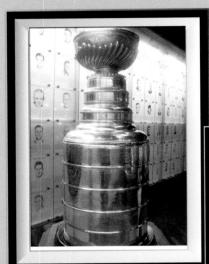

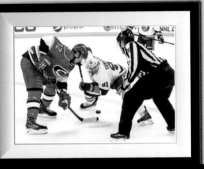

CHAPTER 1

ICE HOCKEY'S GREATEST MOMENTS

There is a good reason that great hockey players are not found traditionally in places where the weather is warm. Hockey was born outside on frozen ponds, lakes, and canals. Even though the game has moved inside, hockey still mostly thrives in places where you can make a rink in your own backyard.

Although National Hockey League (NHL) playoff heroes are forged in June, the sport is part of the culture only in places where rinks can be formed overnight in February. All across Canada, where the game originated, and into states like Minnesota, Michigan, and Massachusetts, a midwinter cold snap means endless days of nonstop pickup games for kids who do not care if they can no longer feel their toes.

The game has changed a lot over the years and is now a serious business from peewee hockey all the way up through junior. Competition in hockey hotbeds is at a peak, with parents spending thousands on the latest gear and travel expenses and getting up to make 5:30 a.m. practice times.

Those kids who show true promise get noticed early as amateur scouts start tracking potential as early as age 14. For exceptional talents, it can be as young as 12. Those kids who show the fortitude to stick with it do so because they love the sport. For every Connor McDavid, John Tavares, or Steven Stamkos, however, there is a player like Bryan Helmer, who retired in 2013 after 20 years in the professional minor leagues. Despite never playing more than 40 games in an NHL season and being signed, released, or traded at least 10 times, he loved the game enough to stick it out through more than 1,000 minor league games to become the top-scoring defenseman in the history of the American Hockey League.

Hockey is a game that teaches perseverance, toughness, and humility. It is a true team sport that requires everyone to be working hard to succeed. The hard work, dedication, and passion of the best players in the game have produced great moments on the ice that fans will tell stories about forever.

The Great Comeback

In a best-of-seven series, a 3–0 lead is a firm stranglehold. At the end of the 2015 season, 181 playoff series had been led three games to none. Out of these, only four times (about 2 percent) has the trailing team come back to win. Only one time has it happened with the Stanley Cup on the line.

In 1942, the Toronto Maple Leafs were ahead 2–0 in game three of the Stanley Cup Final against Detroit, only to blow it and lose 5–2. This put them down 3–0 in the series. Leafs coach Hap Day gambled and benched his top line wingers for two rookies in game four. Tied 3–3 in the third period, one of those rookies, Don Metz, scored the winning goal. Metz then scored a hat trick the next game, a 9–3 win. Turk Broda got the shutout in game six, and the Leafs pulled off a miracle comeback with a 3–1 win in game seven.

Five Straight Cups

Eighteen years later, the Leafs found themselves in the final again and in similar circumstances. This time, the Leafs trailed the Montréal Canadiens 3-0, but no one was surprised. The Canadiens team they faced in 1960 is one of the greatest in the history of the NHL and had won the last four Stanley Cups. Led by the future Hall of Famer Maurice "Rocket" Richard, the Canadiens closed out the series easily in game four with a 4–0 shutout.

This was the first time that a team had won five Cups in a row, a record that has never been matched. Besides the captain, Richard, who retired after the series, Montréal also boasted Richard's brother Henri, Jean Béliveau, Doug Harvey, Bernie Geoffrion, and goalie Jacques Plante on the roster, all of whom are Hall of Famers. This was also Montréal's sixth Cup win in eight years, making it a bona fide dynasty.

Orr Takes Flight

In 1970, Boston Bruin defenseman Bobby Orr had a season for the ages. He won the Hart, Norris, Ross, and Smythe trophies. He led the league in assists (87) and points (120) as a defenseman. He also scored 33 regular season goals as well as a career-high nine in the playoffs. One of those nine playoff goals is perhaps the most famous in NHL history.

In the 1970 Stanley Cup Final, Orr and the Bruins faced St. Louis and were having little trouble with the Blues, leading the series 3–0 after outscoring St. Louis 16–4 in the first three games. The Blues put up a fight in game four, however, and the game went into overtime tied 3–3. When Orr scored the Cup-winning goal against the Blues' Glenn Hall, he was tripped on the play and launched parallel to the ice in celebration. Photographer Ray Lussier captured the moment in one of the sport's most iconic photos.

"Henderson has scored for Canada"

Two years later, Orr played for Team Canada in the 1972 Summit Series against an all-star team from the Soviet Union. The idea behind the series was to pit the world's two best hockey-playing nations against each other in a test for ultimate hockey supremacy.

The Soviets won three of the first five games, Canada won one, and one was tied. So the eight-game series stood at 3-1-1 for Russia going into game six. Canada won that game and the next to force a deciding game eight. The game was back and forth until the Russians took a 5–3 lead at the end of the second period. But in the third, goalie Ken Dryden shut the door, and Phil Esposito and Yvan Cournoyer scored to tie it. Then, with just 34 seconds left, Paul Henderson scored his famous goal off his own rebound to win the series and become a Canadian legend.

The Miracle on Ice

The most famous moment in American international hockey history came on February 22, 1980, in Lake Placid, New York. It was the semifinal game in the 1980 Winter Olympic ice hockey tournament in which the United States played the Soviet Union. Most experts expected the Soviets to demolish the less-experienced Americans. The Soviets had won the last four Olympic gold medals, losing only one Olympic hockey game since 1960.

The Americans were mostly college kids and the youngest team in the tournament. But they had played well under coach Herb Brooks to this point. As expected, the Soviets dominated and led 3-2 going into the third. But goals by Mark Johnson and captain Mike Eruzione gave the United States a 4-3 lead with 10 minutes to go. Broadcaster Al Michaels famously asked and answered, "Do you believe in miracles? Yes!" as the clock ticked down on the victory. The United States beat Finland two days later to win the gold.

The Guarantee

When the United States beat the Soviets in the 1980 Olympics, there was no guarantee they would win gold. They still had to beat Finland. That's the same burden New York Ranger captain Mark Messier placed on his New York Rangers during the Eastern Conference Finals of the 1994 Stanley Cup playoffs. The Rangers trailed New Jersey three games to two, and Messier was looking to give his team a spark.

"We know we have to win it. We can win it, and we are going to win it," Messier guaranteed the media before game six. Messier put the pressure squarely on himself and then delivered in spectacular fashion. Trailing 2-1 in the third period, Messier scored three goals to clinch a 4-3 win, backing up his guarantee with a hat trick. The Rangers then won game seven in double overtime and next beat Vancouver for New York's first Cup win in 54 years.

Bourque Gets His Cup

Messier, one of the greatest players in NHL history, won six Stanley Cups in his storied career. Twenty-one years into his equally impressive career, Colorado Avalanche defenseman Ray Bourque had yet to win a single Cup. He accepted a trade from Boston to Colorado the previous season, 1999–2000, hoping to win his first, but the Avalanche lost in the Conference Finals.

In 2000–2001, Bourque had his best season in six years, scoring 59 points to help the Avalanche win the President's Trophy as the top team in the league. This time, the top-seeded Avalanche beat St. Louis in the Conference Finals to advance against defending champion New Jersey in the Stanley Cup Finals. In a very competitive series, Colorado prevailed in seven games. When Colorado captain Joe Sakic received the Cup from the commissioner, he turned and immediately handed it to Bourque, who was a champion at last. Bourque retired after that final series.

SIDNEY CROSBY
SCORED OT GOAL IN 2010 GOLD MEDAL GAME

HD

Crosby Is Golden

Sidney Crosby won his first Stanley Cup in 2009, in just his fourth year in the NHL. That win in June 2009 was the start of a remarkable nine-month stretch in Crosby's career. In February of 2010, he was selected to represent Canada at the Winter Olympic Games. Canada was heavily favored to win the tournament but did lose one game in the preliminary rounds, 5–3, to the Americans.

The United States and Canada were clearly the two best teams as each country fielded squads with a full complement of NHL stars. The two teams eventually would meet in the gold medal game, which went to overtime tied 2–2. In overtime, Crosby picked up a rebound in the U.S. zone and worked a give-and-go along the left boards with Jarome Iginla. Crosby was able to get a step on defenseman Brian Rafalski, take the return pass, and slide it between goalie Ryan Miller's legs to win the gold.

📖 Words to Understand:

crude: very simple and basic, done in a way that does not show a lot of skill

amateur: a person who does something (such as a sport or hobby) for pleasure and not as a job

disband: to end an organization or group

franchises: a team that is a member of a professional sports league

CHAPTER 2

THE ORIGINS OF ICE HOCKEY

Modern ice hockey is a sport that was developed in eastern Canada and refined in Montréal, Canada, in the 1870s. The game itself, however, traces back in history for centuries.

STICKS AND BALLS

Examples of games where a stick is used to strike a ball along the ground date back to ancient Greece. Carved in marble in the acropolis in Athens is a depiction of two men holding sticks with a ball in play between them. This artwork is at least 2,500 years old.

The game evolved over the years, taking different forms in different regions. In the 13th century, the Irish developed hurling, and the Scots played shinty. Two hundred years prior, people played beikou in China. Ball and stick games like these also developed in Chile, Australia, Russia, and Scandinavia.

LET'S CALL IT HOCKEY

The exact origin of the word hockey is a mystery. There are theories as to where it may have originated. One says that it comes from the French word hoquet, which was the name for a shepherd's staff. These staffs have curved ends and do indeed look like hockey sticks.

Other theories include French explorers hearing Iroquois say a word that sounded like ho gee while playing a stick and ball game or that early pucks were made from the cork bungs of beer barrels that contained Hock ale, a drink commonly referred to as hocky.

HITTING THE ICE

Crude skates made with animal bones have been discovered in Scandinavia that date back 5,000 years. The Dutch are credited with inventing metal skates, which happened in the early 1600s. Who put skating and hockey together? That is the subject of debate. Various paintings and letters from late 18th-century England depict or describe games that look like early versions of hockey and even refer to the activity as "hockey." The idea for a stick and ball game on ice likely came across the Atlantic on English ships to Canada.

Evidence of some version of the game being played from Great Bear Lake to West Virginia exists, and several Canadian cities, including Kingston, Ontario, and Windsor, Nova Scotia, claim to have hosted the first modern hockey game. Wherever the truth may lie, what cannot be disputed is that the game developed in Montréal.

GAME ONE

The first organized hockey game was played at the indoor Victoria Skating Rink in Montréal between two nine-man teams comprised of students from nearby McGill University.

The rules were a mishmash of those from field hockey, polo, and lacrosse. The game became popular at the university, and by 1881, a formal hockey club had formed at McGill. The Victoria rink had formed a club as well.

CARNIVAL GAMES

Two years later, in 1883, the first-ever ice hockey tournament took place at the Montréal Winter Carnival. This gave the game exposure it had not previously experienced, and the interest it drew led to the spread of organized games. By 1886, the five-team Amateur Hockey Association of Canada (AHAC) had formed, with three clubs from Montréal and one each from Ottawa and Quebec City.

Among the rules employed by the new association were no intentional contact and stopping play when the puck went behind the net. There was one on-ice official, and the game began with teams using nine men. When the circumstance arose where players were unavailable for a game, two teams played a game with seven on a side, and the much-improved play that resulted led to this change becoming permanent. The seven positions were goalkeeper, point, cover point, rover, right wing, left wing, and center. The rover position would be removed in 1911, leaving the modern-day six-man lineup.

On March 3, 1875, the first recorded indoor ice hockey game took place at the Victoria Skating Rink in Montréal, Canada.

LORD STANLEY'S CUP

By 1892, the entertaining, fast-paced game had quickly spread across the country, all the way to the central prairies. Canada's governor general at the time, Lord Stanley of Preston, recognized the game's popularity and offered to sponsor a trophy that would be presented to the AHAC champions. Today, the trophy is known as the Stanley Cup and is the oldest known award given for professional athletics in North America.

The 1st Stanley Cup

The Montréal Hockey Club faced the Ottawa Capitals in the very first Stanley Cup game in 1894. Five thousand fans watched Montréal win 3-1, and the game was reported on in the *Montréal Gazette*.

In 1896, the Cup trustees allowed teams from other leagues to challenge the AHAC champion for the trophy. By 1904, no less than five **amateur** hockey leagues were competing for the Cup. In what became known as the Challenge Cup era, teams from towns big and small won the Stanley Cup. The Montréal Wanderers began the tradition of inscribing all team member names on the Cup in 1906. The team from the smallest town to capture the trophy was the 1907 Kenora Thistles, from a town of just 10,000. By 1908, there were both professional and amateur leagues operating, and the Stanley Cup became exclusively a professional championship trophy (the Allan Cup was introduced for amateur champions). The first U.S.-based Stanley Cup winners were the 1917 Seattle Metropolitans.

THE NATIONAL HOCKEY LEAGUE

The year 1917 is significant in hockey history. In November of that year, an organization of professional teams called the National Hockey League (NHL) was formed in Montréal. The league's first president was 30-year-old Frank Calder, a teacher and sportswriter by trade. He ran the NHL for 26 years. The trophy awarded today to the top rookie in the league each year is named in his honor.

Frank Calder, president of the National Hockey League from 1917–1943

The new league had four teams: the Montréal Canadiens, Montréal Wanderers, Ottawa Senators, and Toronto Arenas. Games for the new league began one month later, on December 19, 1917. In January, the Montréal Arena burned down, forcing the Wanderers to **disband**. The Canadiens were able to move to a new arena, and the league continued with three teams. Toronto was the NHL champion that first year, but the Stanley Cup was not an NHL trophy. They beat the Pacific Coast Hockey Association (PCHA) champions, the Vancouver Millionaires, to win the Cup.

THE PROFESSIONAL LEAGUES

In 1919, the Canadiens were again NHL champions and again faced the PCHA champion for the Cup. With the series against Seattle tied after game six, the competition was canceled due to a deadly flu outbreak. This resulted in the Stanley Cup not being awarded, one of only two times that has ever happened. The Quebec Bulldogs joined the NHL for the 1919–1920 season, giving the league four teams, including the Toronto St. Patricks, which replaced the Arenas. This was the Bulldogs' only season as the team relocated to Hamilton, Ontario, and became the Tigers the following year.

Professional leagues continued to form. Besides the PCHA, most notably there was the Western Canada Hockey League (WCHL), which was established in 1921. The NHL champion, however, continued to dominate western competition, with either Toronto or Ottawa winning the Cup for the NHL from 1920 to 1923.

NHL EXPANSION

In 1924, the NHL added two teams to get to six total. This included a second team in Montréal, the Maroons, and the Boston Bruins, the first American-based team. That year, the PCHA folded, and its assets were absorbed by the WCHL. The WCHL's Victoria Cougars won the Cup in 1925. The league then had to restructure as the Western Hockey League for the 1925-1926 season but ended up folding in 1926. This left the NHL as the only league playing for the Stanley Cup.

The first Bruins team to hit the ice in 1924-1925 finished with a league worst 6-24 record.

In that 1925–1926 season, the Hamilton team relocated to become the New York Americans. The Pittsburgh Pirates also joined to give the league three American teams. For 1926–1927, three more U.S. teams joined the NHL: the New York Rangers, Chicago Blackhawks, and Detroit Cougars. The league now had 10 teams, with six in the United States. Also that year, the Toronto St. Patricks were sold to another local group and renamed the Maple Leafs (after a military regiment—the name is a proper noun, and, therefore, the plural is Leafs rather than Leaves).

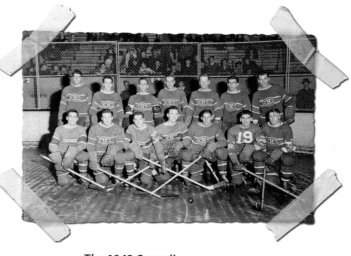

The 1942 Canadiens

NEW RULES

The league was growing, and the way the game was played had to grow with it. Brothers Frank and Lester Patrick, original founders of the PCHA, were pioneers in advancing the sport. Frank played for and coached the Vancouver Millionaires, and Lester coached the Victoria Cougars. Both men won Stanley Cups with their teams.

In 1911, Frank Patrick instituted the use of a blue line along with unlimited substitutions, numbered uniforms, the penalty shot, and a playoff system—all of which were eventually adopted by the NHL.

THE UNLIKELY BACKUP

In 1928, Frank's brother Lester was coach of the Rangers in the Stanley Cup Finals against the Maroons. In game two, Ranger goalie Lorne Chabot was injured and unable to continue in the game. At this time in NHL history, there were no backup goalies. The coach did what he had to do—Patrick put on Chabot's equipment and went in between the pipes himself.

The game went into overtime, and Montréal was unable to beat Patrick, who held on until his team scored to get him the win. The Rangers went on to win the series for their first Stanley Cup.

THE GREAT DEPRESSION

The loss in the Stanley Cup Final to New York was a black day for the Maroons, but things got worse for the club on Black Tuesday, October 24, 1929. On this day, the U.S. stock market crashed, plunging the continent into the Great Depression. The Maroons were one of several **franchises** that would not survive, folding in 1938.

In 1930, the Pittsburgh Pirates moved to Philadelphia, and were renamed the Quakers, but folded the next year. Detroit changed its name from Cougars to Falcons. In 1932, the Falcons changed the name again, this time to the now familiar Red Wings. The Ottawa Senators moved to St. Louis, and became the Eagles, but folded the next year. When the Maroons folded, the NHL was back down to just seven teams.

THE ORIGINAL SIX

In 1942, financial pressure claimed another victim as the New York Americans folded 16 seasons after moving from Hamilton. That left six teams—the Montréal Canadiens, Toronto Maple Leafs, Detroit Red Wings, Chicago Blackhawks, Boston Bruins, and New York Rangers, which would collectively become known as the Original Six.

Text-Dependent Questions:

1. What are the different theories as to where the word "hockey" may have originated?

2. What is the name of the trophy that is the oldest known award given for professional athletics?

3. Who instituted the use of a blue line along with unlimited substitutions, numbered uniforms, the penalty shot, and a playoff system?

Research Project:

Go online and look up old pictures of players and their equipment over the years. Compare and contrast how the equipment has changed.

Hobart Amory Hare "Hobey" Baker

📖 **Words to Understand:**

exhibition game: an unofficial game played under regular game conditions between professional teams

diminutive: exceptionally or notably small

flamboyant: having a very noticeable quality that attracts a lot of attention

inaugural: happening as the first one in a series of similar events

CHAPTER 3

FOR THE LOVE OF THE GAME

When Hobey Baker, the grandfather of American hockey, became captain of the hockey team at Princeton University in New Jersey, he had already dedicated countless hours to becoming one of the best hockey players on the continent. The year was 1910, and professional hockey was not exactly a viable career option. Baker's dedication came from love of the game.

Baker exhibited a skill at a level far beyond his teammates and competitors. The Philadelphia native was a natural stick handler who had no need to look down at the ice once he had the puck on his blade. He was so good, in fact, that wherever he played, people assumed he must be Canadian.

A LEGACY OF COURAGE

As talented as he was, and despite being renowned on the amateur circuit after winning a national amateur championship with St. Nicholas of New York in 1915, Baker chose to make his living in the U.S. Air Force instead of on the ice. He served as a combat pilot in World War I from the summer of 1917 until he was killed during a test flight mishap in December 1918.

Today, the Hobey Baker Award is given to the National Collegiate Athletic Association (NCAA) Division I men's hockey player deemed most outstanding in the country. At Princeton, the Hobey Baker Trophy is given to the freshman player who "in play, sportsmanship, and influence has contributed most to the sport."

GEORGES VÉZINA

When it comes to professional hockey trophies, no player was less likely to have one named for him than Chicoutimi, Quebec's Georges Vézina. That's because Vézina was 18 before he ever learned to skate. Legend has it that Vézina played goal in his boots for his hometown club.

Joseph Georges Gonzague Vézina

Five years after trading his boots for skates, Vézina's team played an **exhibition game** against the Montréal Canadiens in 1910, and he shut them out. The Canadiens signed him as their goalie for the next 16 years. In 1916, he led the club to a Stanley Cup. He never missed a single game in his career, but in 1925 he was feeling dizzy during a game against Pittsburgh and had to come out of the game. He was diagnosed with tuberculosis and died four months later, having never played again. The league established a trophy in his honor the following season, awarded to the most outstanding goaltender in the NHL each season.

Howard William Morenz

HOWIE MORENZ

Vézina's teammate Howie Morenz was hockey's first true superstar. The **diminutive** (5'9", 1.8 m) center's greatest asset was his speed. Dubbed the "Stratford Streak" after his hometown of Stratford, Ontario, he starred for the Canadiens for 12 seasons, leading them in scoring seven straight years.

Off the ice, Morenz had a **flamboyant** personality. Known throughout the league as a fashion plate, he would change his clothes up to three times a day. He loved to play the ponies, spending much of his off-season at the track. He often entertained teammates with ukulele performances.

On the ice, Morenz was the talk of fans around the league. He led the NHL in scoring twice and was a three-time all-star and three-time Hart Trophy winner as league most valuable player (MVP). Morenz also led Montréal to three Stanley Cups.

In January of 1937 in a game against Chicago, Morenz went into the corner with the Blackhawks Earl Seibert. The two collided, with Seibert falling on Morenz's leg. The leg snapped in four places, ending his career. Morenz died in the hospital five weeks later due to complications. Teammate Aurele Joliat speculated on the cause of Morenz's death, saying that when Morenz learned he would never again play the game he loved, he "died of a broken heart." Fifty thousand people attended his funeral at the Montréal Forum.

MORENZ'S LEGACY

Morenz is credited as the reason ice was installed at New York's Madison Square Garden after a promoter saw him play in Montréal. He was the "Babe Ruth of hockey." The Canadiens retired Morenz's number seven sweater, the first player to be so honored. In 1945, eight years after his death, he was one of the nine members in the **inaugural** class of the Hockey Hall of Fame. His daughter, Marlene, married Canadiens star Bernie Geoffrion, and Morenz's grandson and great-grandson have also gone on to play for Montréal.

Foster Hewitt

SMYTHE AND HEWITT

Morenz played the second half of his career during the Great Depression, a time that saw the NHL shrink from 10 to 7 teams as many clubs struggled financially. But in Toronto, Conn Smythe, who purchased the Toronto franchise in 1927 and changed the name from St. Patricks to Maple Leafs, was able to scrape together about $1.8 million for a new arena.

Smythe called the building, completed in 1931, Maple Leaf Gardens, home to the franchise for the rest of the century. Smythe was coach of the team from 1927 to 1930 and was general manager until 1957. He also ran the management company for the arena and hired H. A. Hewitt as the Gardens' general manager and Hewitt's son Foster as the arena's broadcast announcer.

Hewitt's radio broadcasts of Maple Leaf games became legendary. His "Hello Canada, and hockey fans in the United States and Newfoundland" sign-on was the signature of his "Hockey Night in Canada" broadcasts, which aired on television beginning in 1952. His trademark goal call—"He shoots! He scores!"—echoed through Canadian homes across the country on Saturday nights for 57 years. Hewitt was such a legend that Blackhawk great Bobby Hull once described his first encounter with Hewitt by saying, "It was like meeting God." Hewitt was inducted into the Hockey Hall of Fame in 1965.

Maple Leaf Gardens is a historic building located in Toronto, Ontario, Canada

Text-Dependent Questions:

1. Who is the grandfather of American hockey?

2. Which Montréal Canadiens player had a trophy named after him after dying of tuberculosis?

3. Who is the radio broadcaster known for his "Hello Canada, and hockey fans in the United States and Newfoundland" sign-on for his "Hockey Night in Canada" broadcasts?

Research Project:

Look up a list of the Hobey Baker Award recipients over the years and choose a player to further research and learn about his career past college.

The Conn Smythe Trophy is awarded annually to the player judged most valuable to his team (MVP) during the NHL Stanley Cup playoffs.

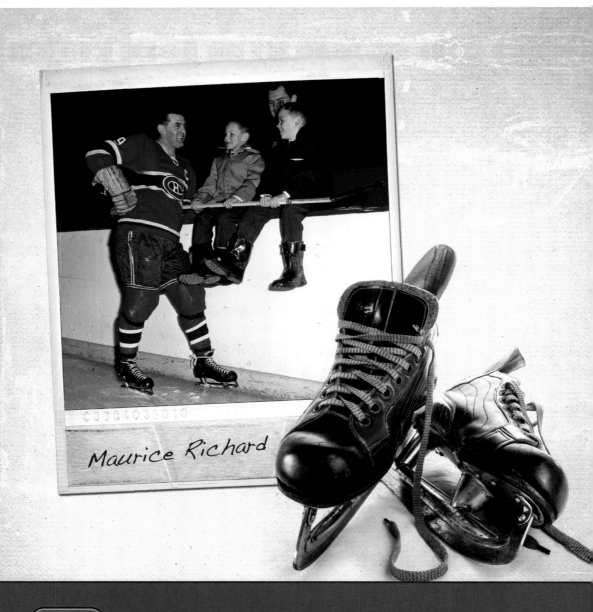

Maurice Richard

Words to Understand:

cadre: a group of people having some unifying relationship

attributes: usually good qualities or features that someone or something has

consummate: very good or skillful

reverence: honor or respect that is felt for or shown to (someone or something)

CHAPTER 4

ON THE SHOULDERS OF GIANTS

Howie Morenz may have been the sport's first superstar, but it was the cadre of greats that followed him that truly built the foundation of the modern game.

THE ROCKET

Maurice "Rocket" Richard was born in the cradle of the game, Montréal, in 1921. A natural athlete and a fierce competitor, he excelled at many sports in his youth, such as boxing and baseball. Hockey, however, was his passion, and he pursued it with an intensity not seen in his personality outside the rink. At 21, he realized his dream of donning the sweater of his hometown Canadiens.

By his third season, Richard had established himself as one of the best players in the league. Coming off a 54-point effort the previous season (seasons were only 50 games long in 1944), Richard started the 1944-1945 season on a tear. He terrorized opposing goalies all season, eventually breaking Joe Malone's 27-year-old record of 44 goals in a season. He went on to score a total of 50 in 50 games, which only four other players in history have done.

Maurice "Rocket" Richard

GOALS AND GUTS

Richard was called the Rocket due to the speed he generated on his skates. That speed was a key contributor to the staggering goal totals he was able to put up over the years. Though the NHL expanded to 60 games in 1946 and 70 in 1949, Richard never scored 50 in a season again. He did, however, score more than 30 goals nine times in 18 seasons. He was the first player to score 500 NHL goals.

As gifted as he was skill wise, Richard was also tough as nails. Both **attributes** were often most vividly on display during the Stanley Cup playoffs. In 1944, he scored all five of his team's goals in a semifinal series game against Toronto. In the 1952 semifinal against Boston, he smacked his head on the ice in the second period of game seven and was knocked unconscious. He had a six-inch (15-cm) gash over one eye and was carried off the ice to the dressing room while still out cold. Amazingly, he returned for the third period. Bleeding through the bandage on his head, he pulled off an end-to-end rush in a 1-1 game to score the series-winning goal. He would demonstrate this toughness until he retired in 1960.

JACQUES PLANTE

One of Richard's teammates who would eventually join him in the Hall of Fame was goaltender Jacques Plante. Plante is most famous for being the first goalie to regularly wear a mask in games. He made the decision eight years into his career, which up until November 1959 had included getting fractures to his cheekbones, nose, or skull seven times. On November 1 against the Rangers, he took a slap shot to the face that required several stitches. He refused to return to the net without the mask that he wore in practice, which his coach grudgingly allowed, and he wore it from then on. By 1975, so did all NHL goalies.

Joseph Jacques Omer Plante

Besides the mask, Plante also pioneered the goaltender as another puck handler. He would venture behind the net to stop pucks and play them out of the zone or up to his defense. Today, having a goaltender that is adept at handling the puck is considered to be a distinct advantage, a skill initiated by Plante.

JEAN BÉLIVEAU

Another member of those great Montréal teams was the **consummate** captain, Jean Béliveau. Béliveau became the Canadiens captain in 1961, a position he held for a decade. Only Henri Richard and Larry Robinson played more games for Montréal than Béliveau did in his 18 seasons.

The **reverence** of the fans, and indeed Canada itself, for this all-time great, lived well past when Béliveau retired in 1971 after another stellar season. When Béliveau died in 2014, the Canadian prime minister, the premier of Quebec, and the mayor of Montréal, along with two former Canadian prime ministers and dozens of hockey luminaries, attended his funeral. So did 1,500 fans, braving the bitter cold outside the cathedral where the funeral was held to pay respects to a hockey legend.

MR. HOCKEY

Gordie Howe also retired in 1971– the first time. Known as "Mr. Hockey," Howe played 25 legendary seasons with the Detroit Red Wings. He scored 786 goals for Detroit, far and away the most ever at the time. He dominated the league with his skill and physically intimidating style, breaking and setting several offensive records. He was inducted into the Hall of Fame the very next year, 1972. In 1973, however, both his sons, Mark and Marty, were set to begin playing in the World Hockey Association (WHA), a new pro league competing against the NHL. Howe still had passion for the game and the ability to play it. So when he had the opportunity to play professionally with his boys, he could not resist.

All three Howes joined the Houston Aeros in 1973 and played together for six seasons, moving to New England to play for the WHA's Whalers in 1977. When the WHA merged with the NHL in 1979, the team survived to become the Hartford Whalers, and Howe played one more season with his boys at age 51. He still managed to score 15 goals and 41 points. In 2011, he attended Mark's Hall of Fame induction.

Gordon "Gordie" Howe

THE GOLDEN JET

Bobby Hull was a teammate of the Howes during Gordie's final season in 1979–1980. Hull would retire that same year, able to play in only nine games for Hartford. Hull was known as "The Golden Jet" due to the way his blonde hair flowed behind him on his high-speed rushes down the left wing. Most of those rushes came in the 1960s during his heyday with the Chicago Blackhawks. With his lethal shot, Hull scored more than 30 goals 13 years in a row.

Only Richard and Geoffrion had scored 50 goals in a season before Hull did it in 1966, scoring 54. In 1972, he became the highest-paid player in history when he took $1 million signing bonus to leave Chicago and play for Winnipeg in the WHA. He was the league's biggest star until he was injured in 1978. Due to injury, he played a total of only 31 games over his final two professional seasons.

BOBBY ORR

Injury was also the reason for the abbreviated career of Boston's Bobby Orr, but what a career it was. No one has ever changed the game like Orr did when he exploded into the league in 1966. Orr won the Calder Trophy that season as Rookie of the Year, but that was just a beginning. A defenseman, he scored more than 30 goals five times, and more than 100 points six times, astounding totals for any player but especially at that position.

While a capable defender and an excellent penalty killer, Orr's biggest impact was made by his freewheeling style from the back end. He influenced millions of young hockey players and dozens of future NHLers, like Paul Coffey, Al MacInnis, Ray Bourque, and Phil Housely. Knee injuries ended Orr's career at age 30 after playing parts of just 12 seasons. Only eight times did he play more than 60 games. It is staggering to imagine what the record books would have looked like had a healthy Orr played 20 seasons.

Robert Gordon "Bobby" Orr

EXPANSION

Star players like Howe, Hull, and Orr, along with other greats like Phil Esposito, Glenn Hall, and Guy Lafleur, increased the popularity of the game across the continent—and not just in traditional hockey playing regions. In 1967, the league added teams in Philadelphia, Pittsburgh, and Minneapolis, but also in St. Louis, Oakland, and Los Angeles. The Original Six had doubled to 12. In 1970, Buffalo and Vancouver joined the league, followed by the New York Islanders and Atlanta Flames in 1972 and then the Washington Capitals and Kansas City Scouts in 1974, and more teams were soon to come.

Text-Dependent Questions:

1. What is Maurice Richard's nickname and why?

2. Which player's funeral attracted the Canadian prime minister, the premier of Quebec, and the mayor of Montréal, along with two former Canadian prime ministers?

3. How did Bobby Orr's career end?

Research Project:

Bobby Orr is credited with influencing millions of young hockey players and dozens of future NHLers, like Paul Coffey, Al MacInnis, Ray Bourque, and Phil Housely. Do some research to examine Orr's influence on the defense position and on the game of hockey in general.

Wayne Gretzky was given the honor of lighting the Olympic flame, which burned bright in the B.C. Place Stadium at the 2010 Winter Olympics in Vancouver, Canada.

Words to Understand:

elusive: cleverly or skillfully evasive

effigy: a crude figure meant to represent a hated person

rookie: a first-year player in a professional sport

lockout: a situation in which an employer tries to force workers to accept certain conditions by refusing to let them come to work until those conditions are accepted

CHAPTER 5

THE MODERN GAME

Most of the expansion teams thrived, especially in Philadelphia, where the Flyers won back-to-back Stanley Cups in 1974 and 1975. As the saying goes, success breeds imitation, which led to the founding of the WHA. When the NHL merged with the WHA in 1979, it gained four teams—the Winnipeg Jets, Quebec Nordiques, Hartford Whalers, and Edmonton Oilers. Playing for the Oilers in his first professional season in 1978-1979 was 18-year-old Wayne Gretzky, and the Oilers' inclusion in the new 21-team NHL (the Oakland franchise had moved to Cleveland but folded) meant the arrival of a player that would change the game forever.

THE GREAT ONE

Gretzky was a slight, relatively slow player when he arrived in the league in 1979, but he was **elusive** and saw the ice with a vision no one has possessed before or since. In his first season, he led the league in scoring and was named Hart Trophy winner as MVP. Gretzky, who was immediately dubbed "The Great One," was not only skillful at scoring goals himself. He was history's premier playmaker, setting up teammates for goals at a record pace.

Gretzky, the NHL's all-time leading scorer, has 1,963 career assists. His former Oilers teammate Mark Messier is second overall in career scoring, with 1,887 total points. This means that even if Gretzky had never scored a single NHL goal, he would still be the league's all-time leading scorer on the basis of his assists alone. That is the kind of playmaker Gretzky was.

DYNASTY TO DYNASTY

Gretzky led the league in scoring every season from 1981–1982 through 1986–1987. In four of those seasons, he had more assists than the next closest player had total points. In four of those seasons, he scored more than 200 points. In four of those seasons, at least two of his teammates also finished with at least 100 points. And in four of those seasons, the Oilers won the Stanley Cup.

When Gretzky came into the league in 1979–1980, the New York Islanders, led by Mike Bossy, Denis Potvin, and Bryan Trottier, were the NHL's dominant force. The Islanders won the Cup in four straight years, from 1980 to 1983. The 1983 victory was a sweep over Gretzky's Oilers.

Redemption for Gretzky and the Oilers came the following season in a finals rematch against the Islanders. This time, Gretzky was not to be denied, leading the playoffs in scoring as the Oilers won the Cup in five games. Taking the mantle from the Islanders, Edmonton went on to win the Cup three more times in the next four seasons. Gretzky was the leading scorer each time, twice winning the Conn Smythe Trophy as playoff MVP.

THE TRADE

After the 1988 Cup win, the Oiler dynasty came to a screeching halt when cash-strapped Edmonton owner Peter Pocklington traded Gretzky and two teammates to Los Angeles for two players, three first-round draft picks, and $15 million in cash. The hockey world, Canada, and Edmonton were shocked. Pocklington was burned in **effigy** outside the Oiler's arena. A member of the Canadian parliament tried to introduce a measure to have the trade blocked. But ultimately, Gretzky became a King in one of the most influential moments in hockey history. Gretzky instantly raised the profile of the sport in California, especially after he led the Kings to the finals in 1993. The league added teams in San Jose and Anaheim in 1991 and 1993, respectively. By 1995, registered hockey players in California jumped to more than 15,000, a more than 200 percent increase from 1990. Before 1988, a total of five NHL players hailed from California. Since 2008, that number is more than 30, including first-round draft picks Beau Bennett, Emerson Etem, and Kerby Rychel. Gretzky's impact is undeniable and continues to be felt in the sport.

Wayne Gretzky

FRANCHISE MOVEMENT

Besides the additions of San Jose and Anaheim, there were several other changes since the WHA merger. In 1980, the Atlanta Flames moved to Calgary, where they would win a Cup behind Al MacInnis and Doug Gilmour in 1989. The Kansas City franchise had moved to Denver to become the Colorado Rockies in 1976. In 1982, they moved again, this time to New Jersey, becoming the Devils. In 1992, the Ottawa Senators were reborn as an expansion team, entering along with Tampa Bay. The next season, the Florida Panthers were also added, bringing the total number of teams to 26. Gretzky is largely credited with increasing the interest in the sport in nontraditional markets like Anaheim and Florida, making NHL hockey there possible.

FRANCHISE STAYING PUT

Hockey's other great superstar of the era, Mario Lemieux, is widely credited with saving the Pittsburgh Penguins franchise. Lemieux was drafted first overall in 1984. Four inches (10 cm) and 50 lbs. (22.7 kg) bigger than Gretzky, Lemieux was a different type of superstar.

He used his size and strength to drive to the net, and it was very tough to take the puck from him. When he arrived in Pittsburgh, the franchise was at rock bottom. They were averaging less than 7,000 fans per home game and had not had a winning season in five years. Things did not improve in Lemieux's first season. Although he won the Calder as top **rookie** and scored 100 points, the team again lost more than 50 games and finished last in the division.

It would be four years before the team around Lemieux was good enough to qualify for the playoffs. Lemieux had a career year with 85 goals and 199 points. The Penguins lost in the second round but gained valuable experience. After taking a step back and missing the playoffs the next season, when Lemieux missed the last 23 games with an injury, the Penguins finished first in the division in 1990–1991. Lemieux missed the first 56 games, but rookie Jaromir Jagr picked up the slack with 57 points. In the playoffs, Lemieux was unstoppable, leading all playoff scorers with a career-high 44 points to win the Stanley Cup in six games over Minnesota and the Conn Smythe Trophy.

Mario Lemieux

The next season, the Penguins repeated the trick, winning the division and then sweeping Chicago in the finals for their second straight Cup victory. Lemieux led the league in scoring with 131 points and the playoffs in scoring with 34.

A MAGNIFICENT RECOVERY

The next season may have been Lemieux's most magnificent. Despite being diagnosed with Hodgkin's lymphoma and missing 22 games, he scored 160 points to win the scoring title and was named MVP. The Penguins made the playoffs in 11 straight seasons from 1990 to 2000 but never won another Cup with Lemieux. Although Lemieux is unquestionably one of the best offensive players ever to play, injuries devastated his career. He never played a full season in his 17 years. He retired in 1997, plagued by chronic back problems.

In 1998, Lemieux again saved the team, this time leading a group to purchase the bankrupt Penguins in September of 1999. Then, after taking three years off, he returned to the NHL in December of 2000. He played five more seasons but played more than 45 games only once before finally retiring in 2006.

MODERN-DAY DYNASTIES

In the 10 seasons from 1994–1995 to the 2004–2005 season, which was cancelled due to a labor dispute (the only time other than 1919 that the Stanley Cup was not awarded), three franchises won multiple Stanley Cups: the New Jersey Devils, the Colorado Avalanche (relocated from Quebec in 1995), and the Detroit Red Wings. Each franchise won their first Cups of the period in successive years, New Jersey in 1995, Colorado in 1996, and Detroit in

Mario Lemieux's retired number 66 hangs above the scoreboard at Consol Energy Center in Pittsburgh.

1997. New Jersey, dubbed a "Mickey Mouse operation" by none other than Wayne Gretzky after the Oilers beat them 13-4 in 1983, turned the corner when it hired Lou Lamoriello as team president in 1987. Lamoriello then appointed himself general manager of the club and proceeded to assemble a group of core players that he could build around, including Brendan Shanahan, Bill Guerin, Scott Niedermayer, and Martin Brodeur. After Brodeur was named as the starter in goal in 1993, the Devils won the Cup in 1995, 2000, and 2003.

ROY MAKES HIS MARK

The turning point for Colorado came in the middle of the 1996 season when Canadiens goalie Patrick Roy demanded a trade due to conflicts with the new coach in Montréal. He was dealt to a Colorado team that included Joe Sakic and Peter Forsberg. Roy was the final ingredient, leading the team to the Cup win that year and again in 2001.

MOTOWN MAGIC

In Detroit, the all-world Steve Yzerman was the veteran leader of the Red Wings in 1997. The longtime captain led the Wings into the playoffs, where they ran into bitter rivals and defending champions Colorado in the Conference Finals. After a hard-fought six-game series win, Detroit swept Philadelphia in the Cup Final for the win. With future Hall of Famers Shanahan and Nick Lidstrom in tow, Yzerman led the Wings to a repeat win over Washington the next season. Detroit won a third Cup in this window in 2002.

Patrick Roy

SALARY CAP ERA

After the 2004–2005 **lockout**, the league resumed play in 2005–2006 with a hard salary cap in place. In the first 10 seasons under the cap, two franchises prospered with multiple championships.

The Chicago Blackhawks were terrible in 2006 and 2007, and, therefore, they drafted third overall and first overall in the respective years. Chicago nailed both picks, selecting Jonathan Toews and Patrick Kane. The two forwards led Chicago to its first Cup win in 49 years when the Hawks won in 2010. They followed up with two more wins in 2013 and 2015.

Jonathan Toews lifts the Stanley Cup at the Blackhawks victory parade in downtown Chicago 2013.

In Los Angeles, successful drafting yielded center Anze Kopitar and goalie Jonathan Quick in 2005 and defenseman Drew Doughty in 2008. The result was the first and second Stanley Cups in franchise history in 2012 and again in 2014.

Text-Dependent Questions:

1. Which player is dubbed "The Great One"?

2. What happened in 1988 to shock the hockey world?

3. Who is largely credited with saving the Pittsburgh Penguins franchise?

Research Project:

Find information on the Internet about the 2004-2005 lockout and share your opinions on why it happened and the effect it had on professional hockey as a whole.

Sidney Patrick Crosby

Words to Understand:

prospect: someone or something that is likely to succeed or to be chosen

notorious: well-known or famous especially for something bad

draft: a system whereby exclusive rights to selected new players are apportioned among professional teams

backstopped: when a goaltender leads his/her team to victory due to outstanding play

CHAPTER 6

MODERN-DAY STARS

There are many philosophies on what makes the foundation of a good team. Is it a top-flight goaltender? Many say this is the key. Others will say the goaltender can be average or better if the defense in front of him is stellar, so the focus should be the blue line. Still others will contest that success comes from strength up the middle—having great centers that are good at their roles from first line to fourth. Today's NHL is stocked with stars that fit the bill at every position.

UP THE MIDDLE

Mario Lemieux played his final season in the NHL in 2005–2006 alongside the Penguin's first overall **draft** pick, Sidney Crosby. Like Lemieux, Crosby was touted as a "can't miss" **prospect** and a generational player.

Crosby scored 39 goals and 102 points in that rookie season, and with Lemieux retired the next year, he became the youngest captain in league history. He won both the Ross and Hart trophies in each of 2007 and 2014. The five-time all-star led the Penguins to the Stanley Cup in 2009 and has won two Olympic gold medals.

Crosby's teammate on those two gold medal-winning teams from Canada in 2010 and 2014 was Chicago's Jonathan Toews. Toews was drafted third overall the year after Crosby and also was named the youngest captain in his franchise's history at 20.

Toews has scored at least 20 goals in every season and is considered one of the best leaders and top face-off men in the game. Toews won the Stanley Cup and Conn Smythe Trophy as playoff MVP in 2010. His Blackhawks also won the Cup in 2013 and 2015.

One of Crosby's teammates on the Penguins is also a top center in the league and one of the game's best players. Evgeni Malkin was drafted second overall in 2004. Malkin scored 85 points in his 2006–2007 rookie season to win the Calder Trophy.

Malkin scored 113 points to win the scoring title in 2009. He capped the 2009 season by also leading the playoffs in scoring, winning both the Conn Smythe Trophy as playoff MVP and the Stanley Cup. In 2011–2012, he led the league in scoring again, this time adding the NHL MVP award as well.

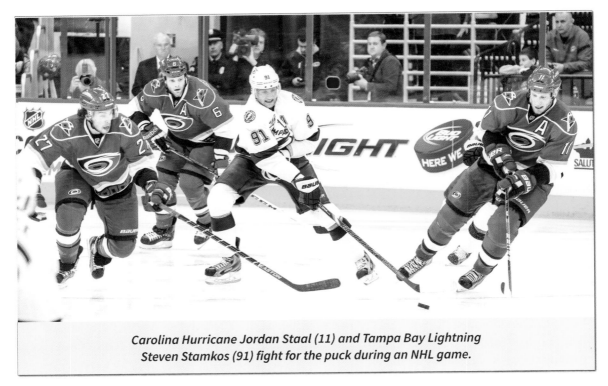

Carolina Hurricane Jordan Staal (11) and Tampa Bay Lightning Steven Stamkos (91) fight for the puck during an NHL game.

Like Crosby, Steven Stamkos was also the first overall pick in the NHL draft, going in 2008 to the Tampa Bay Lightning. Stamkos had scored 100 goals in two seasons in junior hockey.

The goal scoring did not stop when Stamkos got to the NHL. After a good rookie season when he scored 23 goals, he led the league with 51 the following year. This was the first of three straight seasons with more than 90 points. Stamkos also led the league in scoring in 2011–2012.

DOWN THE WING

Corey Perry was drafted in the first round by Anaheim in 2003 and joined the Ducks in 2005. He has five 30-goal seasons under his belt, including 2010–2011, when he led the league with 50 goals and was named Hart Trophy winner as NHL MVP.

Perry also starred as a winger on the Canadian Olympic team for both gold medal wins in 2010 and 2014. He is a five-time NHL all-star.

Another gold medalist from that 2014 Canadian Olympic team was Dallas Stars captain Jamie Benn. Benn was a steal in the 2007 draft for Dallas, taken in the fifth round.

Corey Perry

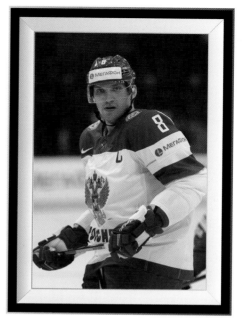

Alexander Ovechkin

Benn made the Stars roster in 2009 and blossomed in the 2013–2014 season. He was named captain, scored 34 goals, and made his first All-Star Team while winning the gold on the Olympic stage. In the next season, Benn was even better, winning the Art Ross Trophy for leading the league in scoring and going to the All-Star Game again.

Alexander Ovechkin was the complete opposite of Benn on draft day in terms of expectations. Ovechkin, a Russian, was the "can't miss" number one prospect in the 2004 draft, and the Washington Capitals took him with the first pick.

Ovechkin was even better than advertised when he debuted in 2005, scoring 51 goals and 106 points to win Rookie of the Year over Crosby. He has scored more than 50 goals six times and has never scored less than 30. He is a five-time all-star but has never been to a Stanley Cup Final.

Another stellar first overall pick was Chicago winger Patrick Kane. The American-born Kane was the top pick in the 2007 draft, and made an impact right away, scoring 72 points to win the Calder Trophy as a 19-year-old.

Kane has been even better since. The five-time all-star has helped to lead the Blackhawks to three Stanley Cups, including in 2010, when he scored the Stanley Cup-winning goal in overtime against Philadelphia. It was Chicago's first Cup win in 49 years.

Drew Doughty

Duncan Keith

AT THE POINT

Two-time Stanley Cup champion Drew Doughty was taken second overall behind Stamkos in the 2008 NHL draft by the Los Angeles Kings. Doughty made the Kings as a rookie defenseman and broke out the following season, making his first All-Star Team and registering a career-high 59 points.

In 2011–2012, Doughty led all playoff performers with 12 assists in the postseason, and the Kings won the franchise's first-ever Stanley Cup. Two years later, the Kings won the Cup again. Doughty also has two Olympic gold medals from 2010 and 2014.

Those Canadian Olympic teams that won back-to-back gold medals were stocked with talent on the blue line. Shea Weber was one of the team's best in 2010, named to the tournament All-Star Team. He also has been an NHL all-star five times since he debuted with Nashville in 2006.

Weber's blistering shot has been tracked at more than 108 miles per hour (174 km/h). He has used it to score more than 15 goals in a season seven times. Only once has he played less than 78 games while logging well over 25 minutes of ice time every game against the opposition's best players.

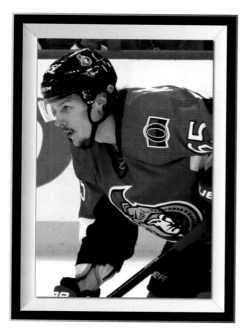

Erik Karlsson

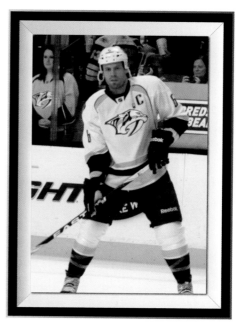

Shea Weber

Weber's partner on those Canadian Olympic teams was Chicago's Duncan Keith, another **notorious** minutes muncher. The Blackhawks took Keith in the second round in 2002, and he made the team in 2005.

In 2009–2010, Keith scored a career-high 69 points to win the Norris Trophy as best defensemen while helping the Hawks win their first Stanley Cup. The five-time all-star was a key contributor to another Cup-winning run in 2013. Keith won the Norris again in 2014 and a third Cup in 2015 when he also won the Conn Smythe as playoff MVP.

Ottawa chose Erik Karlsson in 2008 in the middle of the first round. Four defensemen were taken in the top five, including Doughty, and six in total were drafted before Karlsson. Among the seven defensemen taken in the top 15, there are two Norris Trophy seasons. Both of those belong to Karlsson.

Karlsson grew up playing in Sweden, like all-time great defensemen Nicklas Lidstrom and Börje Salming. He joined the Senators in 2009, and in 2011–2012, he scored 78 points to become an all-star and Norris winner. He accomplished both feats again in 2014–2015.

BETWEEN THE PIPES

Karlsson's countryman and New York Ranger goalie Henrik Lundqvist is one of the best goalies in the world. He was their seventh-round pick in 2000, 205th overall. He debuted in 2005 and set an NHL record by winning at least 30 games in each of his first seven seasons. Lundqvist won the Vézina Trophy as top goalie in 2012 and has been in the top six in Vézina voting in every season of his career.

Like Karlsson, he honed his craft in Sweden, which Lundqvist plays for internationally. In 2006, he **backstopped** the Swedes to the Olympic gold medal in Torino, Italy.

Lundqvist won that gold medal against Finland, a nation that has produced world-class goaltenders for most of this century. This includes Tuukka Rask, taken in the first round by Toronto in 2005. Rask never played for Toronto as he was traded to Boston in 2006 in a steal of a deal for the Bruins.

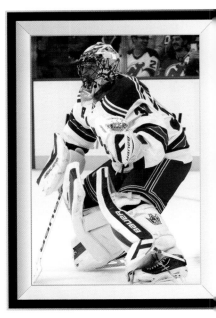

Henrik Lundqvist

Rask led the league in goals against average and save percentage as a rookie in 2009–2010, splitting time with Tim Thomas. Rask served as backup to Thomas when the Bruins won the Stanley Cup in 2011. He was the starter in 2013–2014, leading the league in shutouts on the way to winning the Vézina Trophy.

Rask's countryman Pekka Rinne did not have nearly the same expectations when he was drafted by Nashville. He was selected in the eighth round in 2004, the last year the draft had an eighth round.

Rinne made the most of his opportunity when he debuted as the starter for the Predators full time in 2008 and has been one of the league's top goalies since. In 2010–2011, Rinne posted a career-best .930 save percentage and 2.12 goals against average and was named an all-star. He is a three-time Vézina finalist.

Carey Price won the Vézina Trophy as a member of the Montréal Canadiens in 2015. He had a career-best season that year, leading the league in goals against average (1.96) and save percentage (.933). He also won the Hart Trophy as NHL MVP. This was only the seventh time in league history that a goalie won that award.

This type of success was expected of Price from the day he was drafted fifth overall by Montréal. He has led the league in wins on two occasions. He is also a gold medalist as the goalie for the 2014 Canadian Olympic hockey team.

Text-Dependent Questions:

1. Which player won both the Ross and Hart trophies in each of 2007 and 2014, led the Penguins to the Stanley Cup in 2009, and has won two Olympic gold medals?

2. Which player is a five-time all-star but has never been to a Stanley Cup Final?

3. Who's blistering shot has been tracked at more than 108 miles per hour (174 km/h)?

Research Project:

Compare all the awards each current star has won during his career to date and assess who you think is the Most Valuable Player at each position.

NICKLAS LIDSTRÖM

BOBBY HULL

WAYNE GRETZKY

PHIL ESPOSITO (LEFT)

GORDIE HOWE

JEAN BELIVEAU (RIGHT)

MARIO LEMIEUX (MIDDLE LEFT)

MARTIN BRODEUR

GUY LAFLEUR

HOCKEY HALL OF FAME

MARK MESSIER

The Hockey Hall of Fame is located in Toronto, Canada. The first members were inducted in 1945, although the first actual building for the hall was not opened until 1961. That first class included greats such as Hobey Baker, Howie Morenz, and Georges Vézina. The hall quickly outgrew its original location on the grounds of the Canadian National Exhibition and in 1993 was relocated to Brookfield Place in downtown Toronto. It has been renovated several times since, designed to accommodate new inductees well into the future. More than 260 players, 100 builders, and 15 officials have been enshrined. The hall gets more than 300,000 visitors every year.

Scan here to go to the Hockey Hall of Fame website.

ICE HOCKEY'S GREATEST PLAYERS

Wayne Gretzky scored like no one who has ever laced up skates. Bobby Orr's greatness is undeniable. Mario Lemieux played a game of artistry and grace with the strength of a bull. These are the greats who inspired the current stars of the game.

Gretzky grew up idolizing Gordie Howe. So did Bobby Orr. Howe played so long that he was a favorite of both players even though Orr retired the year before Gretzky's first NHL season. Lemieux admired Guy Lafleur. It goes back to the very beginnings of the game and stars like Richard, Morenz, and Shore.

These great stars hail from Canada, where the sport is akin to a religion, and three-year-olds on skates are dreaming of the NHL. The game also has become an international one, however, with the Hall of Fame admitting players from 16 different European countries, beginning with the great Soviet goaltender Vladislav Tretiak in 1989.

Tretiak never played a minute in the NHL but was recognized for his distinguished international career. Swedish-born Börje Salming was the first European player to be an NHL all-star—he was inducted in 1996. Now, the hall has several European-born superstars who dominated in the NHL. Names like Forsberg, Sundin, and Lidstrom from Sweden; Bure, Fetisov, and Larionov from Russia; and Mikita and Stastny from Slovakia all grace the hall.

Great players are being raised and trained across the world, but most of the game's legends honed their skills in North America. Nine of Canada's 10 provinces and eight American states have sent players to the hall. In 1960, more than 95 percent of NHL players were Canadian. In 2015, that percentage was just above 50.

In the Hall of Fame, Canadians account for 88 percent of inducted players as of 2015. But with more of the world represented in the NHL than ever before, the hall will begin to reflect that the game's greatest players are not just from North America anymore. Only time will tell if these future stars will one day be good enough to be mentioned alongside the current all-time greatest players.

CENTERS

Wayne Gretzky is the best center in the sport's history. Some will argue that Lemieux was better, but Gretzky had better linemates, or lament what might have been if Lemieux avoided injury and illness. Buts and ifs aside, all we have to go on is what happened. Gretzky scored 1.92 points per game, the highest average in history. Gretzky and Lemieux played at a time when league scoring was at an apex, but so did everyone else they played with, and no one approached their numbers.

Wayne Gretzky

Mario Lemieux

Gretzky is the only player ever to score more than 200 points in a season, and he did that four times. He holds more than 60 NHL scoring records, including goals, assists, and points in a season (92, 163, and 215 respectively).

Mario Lemieux came into the league five years after Gretzky and made an immediate impact, scoring on the first shot of the first shift of his career. His best offensive year came in 1988–1989, with 199 points. He won the first of his six scoring titles that season and the first of his three MVPs.

Lemieux was lethal with the man advantage, where he scored nearly 35 percent of his 690 career goals. His most impressive year may have been 1992–1993, when he missed 22 games to undergo treatment for Hodgkin's lymphoma, a type of cancer, and still won the scoring title with 160 points. Only Gretzky has ever averaged more points per game than Lemieux did that magical season.

Some will argue that Gretzky owes a lot of his success to having a teammate like Mark Messier, including Gretzky himself. Messier didn't become a center until the 1984 playoffs when he sparked Edmonton to its second Cup win and won the Conn Smythe Trophy as playoff MVP. The Oilers won two more Cups before Gretzky was traded to L.A. and then a fifth in 1990 with Messier as captain. He was named NHL MVP that season.

He won his second MVP award as captain of the Rangers when he was traded to New York in 1991. He then famously led the Rangers to the 1994 Stanley Cup, his sixth championship. Only Gretzky has more career points than Messier.

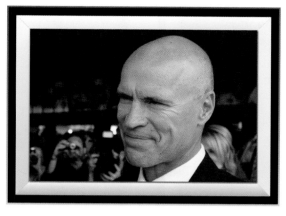

Mark Messier

Gretzky, Lemieux, and Brett Hull are the only players ever to score more goals in a single season than Phil Esposito, who notched 76 in 1970–1971 for the Bruins. That season was the second of six in a row that the eight-time all-star led the league in goals and the first of four in a row Esposito led the league in scoring. He won five Art Ross Trophies in his career.

Phil Esposito

Esposito had a nose for the net like few who have ever played. He is sixth all-time in career goals and 10th in career points. In both 1970 and 1972 he led the playoffs in scoring to help Boston win two Stanley Cups. Esposito won two league MVP awards in his Hall of Fame career.

The outstanding Montréal Canadiens captain Jean Béliveau won only one Hart Trophy as league MVP in his stellar 20-year career, all played with Montréal. That was in 1955–1956 when he led the NHL in goals (47) and scoring (88). The 10-time all-star was, however, valuable to his team every year in so many ways.

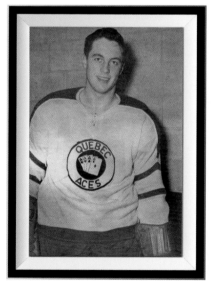

Jean Béliveau

Béliveau was team captain for 10 seasons starting after Doug Harvey left in 1961, the longest tenure in team history. During his captaincy, the Canadiens won five Stanley Cups. He won the Conn Smythe as playoff MVP for the 1965 Cup run. Béliveau also won five straight Stanley Cups before he was captain, from 1956 to 1960, for a total of 10 career championships. Only his teammate Henri Richard won more.

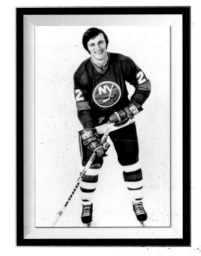

Maurice "Rocket" Richard   *Gordie Howe*   *Mike Bossy*

WINGERS

When Béliveau joined the team full time in 1953, Maurice "Rocket" Richard was the Montréal Canadiens' best player and the top goal scorer in the NHL. Richard led the league in goals that season and the next, the last of five seasons that he did so in his career. Richard was named to 14 consecutive All-Star Teams and won a Hart Trophy as MVP in 1947.

Richard was also a key contributor to eight Stanley Cup Championship runs in his 15 years with Montréal, beginning with a league-leading 12 playoff goals as the Canadiens won the Cup in his rookie year of 1944. He led the playoffs in goals five times in his career and in scoring twice.

Béliveau's career bridged those of Richard and another of Montréal's all-time great wingers, Guy Lafleur. Lafleur debuted as a rookie a few months after Béliveau retired in 1971. In the heart of his career, Lafleur scored more than 100 points in six straight seasons, 1975 to 1980, and was named an all-star in each of those seasons as well. During this stretch, he led the league in scoring for three straight years and won back-to-back Hart Trophies as NHL MVP in 1977 and 1978.

In the playoffs, he was equally dominant. Montréal won four straight Cups from 1976 to 1979, and Lafleur led the playoffs in scoring three times in a row, including 1977, when he won the Conn Smythe as playoff MVP.

When Montréal's run of four straight Cups ended, that of the New York Islanders began. The Islanders won the Cup each year from 1980 to 1983, led by the goal-scoring sensation Mike Bossy. Bossy scored more than 50 goals in all but his final, injury-shortened season when he had 38.

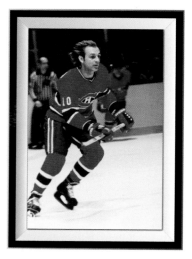

Guy Lafleur

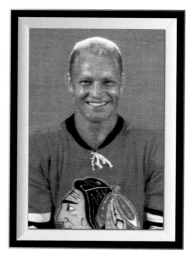

Bobby Hull

Bossy followed up a Calder Trophy-winning season as Rookie of the Year in 1978, with a league-leading 69-goal season in 1979. The next year, the Islanders began their Cup run. For three straight years, Bossy led the playoffs in goals from 1981 to 1983. He led in scoring in 1981 as well, and in 1982 he won the Conn Smythe Trophy as playoff MVP after scoring the Stanley Cup-winning goal.

Twelve-time all-star Bobby Hull retired the year the Islanders won their first Cup. Hull was a prolific goal scorer for the Blackhawks throughout the 1960s, leading the league in goals seven times in the decade. In 1965 and 1966, Hull won back-to-back Hart Trophies as NHL MVP, leading the league in scoring in 1966, one of three seasons in which he accomplished that feat in the 1960s.

Hull's playoff success was limited to one Stanley Cup championship in 1961, although he would lead the playoffs in goals in three other seasons and in scoring in 1965. Hull scored 610 NHL goals and another 303 in the WHA that are not recognized in his official career totals.

Gordie Howe's combined NHL and WHA goal totals would give him 975 combined, the most of any player. Only Gretzky has scored more than the 801 official NHL goals Howe collected in his legendary 26-year career, including one season at age 51.

Howe led the NHL in goals five times, scoring six times, and won six MVPs. He was named to a record 21 All-Star Teams. One of the toughest players in the league throughout his career with Detroit, part of his immense legacy is the "Gordie Howe hat trick," an unofficial stat collected when a player records a goal, an assist, and a major penalty for fighting in he same game. He won four Stanley Cups in Detroit, including 1955, when he led the playoffs in scoring.

DEFENSEMEN

Due to the steady brilliance and length of his career (scoring more than 60 points for 21 straight seasons), there are those who say Howe may be the best player ever, along with Gretzky, Lemieux, and Bobby Orr. Very few would argue that Orr is the best defenseman in history. It was Orr who gave the position an offensive aspect when he debuted with Boston in 1966, winning the Calder Trophy that season. The following season he traded the Calder for the Norris Trophy as best defenseman, which he won a record eight straight times.

Doug Harvey

Orr left an unprecedented legacy. He won three straight Hart trophies, one of only seven defensemen to win the MVP. No other defenseman has led the league in scoring, which Orr did twice.

Orr does not hold the record for most times winning MVP among defensemen. Another Bruin, four-time winner Eddie Shore, holds that honor. Shore played in the 1930s when he was named to eight All-Star Teams. He also won Stanley Cup Championships in 1929 and 1939.

Shore was one of the toughest players in a very violent league. His 165 penalty minutes in 43 games in 1927–1928 were a record for a single season. Hall of Fame teammate Milt Schmidt once said of Shore, "Eddie always went down the middle of the ice. People bounced off him like tenpins." Those collisions led to several altercations, which Shore was happy to entertain. In a 1929 game against the Maroons, he got a record five fighting majors.

Eddie Shore

Another all-time great Bruin defenseman is Ray Bourque, who played for Boston from 1979 to 2000. He entered the league with an all-star level, Calder Trophy-winning season in 1979–1980. He became a fixture as an all-star, getting named 19 times, a record for defensemen.

The heyday of Bourque's career came between 1987 and 1994 when he won five Norris Trophies as the league's best defenseman. Bourque is the NHL's career leader among defensemen in goals, assists, and points. His career-best season came in 1983–1984 when he scored 31 goals and 96 points. Bourque was the best power play defenseman of his era, scoring 42 percent of his goals with the man advantage. His 60-game winning goals are also a record for defensemen.

Orr is the only defenseman to win more Norris Trophies than Doug Harvey. Harvey played 19 total seasons, mostly with Montréal, serving as the Canadiens captain in the 1960–1961 season. He was named to 11 consecutive All-Star Teams. He won his first Norris Trophy and the first of four in a row in 1955. He also won two more Norris Trophies with the Canadiens in 1960 and 1961. During his time in Montréal, the Canadiens won six Stanley Cups.

After the 1961 season, Montréal traded their superstar defenseman to the Rangers in retaliation for Harvey's efforts in working with Detroit star Ted Lindsay to form the NHL Players' Association, a player union. Harvey won a Norris in his first year with New York.

Like Harvey, Detroit Red Wing star Nicklas Lidström won seven Norris Trophies as well, the first non-North American to win it. The Swede captured the award six times in seven years between 2001 and 2008. Lidström became captain of the Red Wings in 2006 after longtime captain, superstar center Steve Yzerman, retired. Lidström was a part of three Red Wings Cup champions captained by Yzerman in 1997, 1998, and then in 2002, when Lidström was named playoff MVP.

After becoming captain, Lidström continued the tradition of leading Detroit to the playoffs, which the Wings made every year of Lidström's career. In his Norris Trophy season in 2008, the captain also led the team to another Cup win. The 12-time all-star won his seventh Norris in 2011.

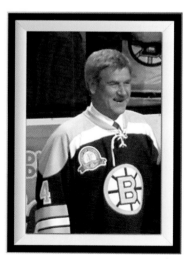
Bobby Orr

Ray Bourque

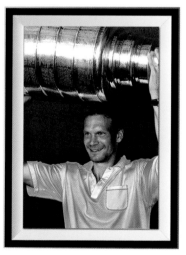
Nicklas Lidström

GOALTENDERS

One of the goaltenders on Lidström's 2002 and 2008 Cup-winning teams was Czech-born Dominik Hašek. Hašek played for four teams in his career but had his greatest team success with the Wings.

Hašek's greatest individual success came with Buffalo from 1992 to 2001. After winning the starting job in 1993, he was the best goaltender in the league for eight years. He led the league in save percentage for six years in a row. Hašek won the Vézina Trophy six times as best goalie. He also won back-to-back Hart Trophies as league MVP in 1997 and 1998, the only time in history this has happened. A six-time all-star, Hašek also had success on the international level, winning gold for the Czech Republic at the 1998 Olympics.

Martin Brodeur knows what it means to win Olympic gold. The Canadian won the gold in Salt Lake City, Utah, in 2002, and in Vancouver in 2010.

At the NHL level, Brodeur played all but seven games with the New Jersey Devils. He won the Calder Trophy as Rookie of the Year in 1994. Brodeur led the league in wins nine times and became the all-time leader in career wins and shutouts. He and Terry Sawchuk are the only goalies with more than 100 shutouts. Brodeur, a seven-time all-star, won four Vézina Trophies in his 22 seasons. Brodeur also had a stellar playoff career as he is the all-time leader in career playoff shutouts and second in wins. He won the Stanley Cup three times.

Patrick Roy is second to Brodeur in career wins by a large margin, 140 behind. In the playoffs, however, Roy is the career leader. He started piling up playoff wins in his rookie season when he surprisingly led Montréal to a Stanley Cup victory in 1986. He won the Conn Smythe Trophy

Jacques Plante

Ken Dryden

Patrick Roy

Martin Brodeur

Dominik Hašek

as playoff MVP. He repeated the trick in 1993, winning MVP again by making more than 600 playoff saves.

Also during his time in Montréal, Roy won three Vézinas and led the league in save percentage four times. The six-time all-star was traded to Colorado in 1995, winning the Cup in his first season there. He won his fourth career Cup in 2001, posting four shutouts to win his third playoff MVP.

Roy is one of a trio of great Montréal Canadiens goaltenders. Before Roy arrived 1986, Montréal had not won a Cup since 1979 when they had Ken Dryden between the pipes. Dryden was a late-season call-up in 1971, playing just six games. But he allowed just nine goals in those games and was named playoff starter. Like Roy, he led Montréal to a Cup victory in his first playoff with the team. He also won the Conn Smythe Trophy as MVP.

Dryden won the Calder the next season after leading the league in wins, the only player to be playoff MVP before Rookie of the Year. He led Montréal to five more Stanley Cups before retiring suddenly after his fifth Vézina season in 1979.

The third in the Canadiens great goalie trio is Jacques Plante. While famous for innovating the goalie mask, Plante was also a spectacular netminder. He led the league in wins five times and won the Vézina five times in a row with Montréal. Plante earned a sixth Vézina along with the Hart Trophy for league MVP when he won a career-high 42 games and led the league in goals against average for the sixth time in 1962.

Plante was traded to the New York Rangers in 1963 and retired in 1965. He made a comeback with the expansion St. Louis Blues team in 1968 as a backup to Hall of Famer Glenn Hall. Plante led the league in goals against average and was awarded his record seventh Vézina.

Career Snapshots

Centers

#4 JEAN BELIVEAU 1950-71

507 goals
712 assists
1219 points

#7 PHIL ESPOSITO 1963-81

717 goals
873 assists
1590 points

#99 WAYNE GRETZKY 1979-99

894 goals
1963 assists
2563 points

#11 MARK MESSIER 1979-2004

694 goals
1193 assists
1887 points

#66 MARIO LEMIEUX 1984-2006

690 goals
1033 assists
1723 points

Wingers

#9 MAURICE "ROCKET" RICHARD 1942-60

544 goals
421 assists
965 points

#9 GORDIE HOWE 1946-80

801 goals
1049 assists
1850 points

#22 MIKE BOSSY 1977-87

573 goals
553 assists
1126 points

#10 GUY LAFLEUR 1971-91

560 goals
793 assists
1353 points

#9 BOBBY HULL 1979-99

610 goals
560 assists
1170 points

*All the above athletes are members of the Hall of Fame

Defensemen

#2 EDDIE SHORE 1926–40

103 goals
176 assists
279 points

#2 DOUG HARVEY 1947–69

88 goals
452 assists
540 points

#4 BOBBY ORR 1966–79

270 goals
645 assists
915 points

#77 RAY BOURQUE 1979–2001

395 goals
1111 assists
1506 points

#5 NICKLAS LIDSTRÖM 1991–2012

264 goals
878 assists
1142 points

Goaltenders

#1 JACQUES PLANTE 1952–73

437 wins
2.38 goals against average
82 shutouts

#29 KEN DRYDEN 1970–79

258 wins
2.24 goals against average
46 shutouts

#33 PATRICK ROY 1984–2003

551 wins
2.54 goals against average
.910 save percentage

#39 DOMINIK HASEK 1990–2008

389 wins
2.20 goals against average
.922 save percentage

#30 MARTIN BRODEUR 1991–2015

691 wins
2.24 goals against average
.912 save percentage

A panoramic view of Malmö Arena in Malmö, Sweden.

Words to Understand:

purists: a person who has very strong ideas about what is correct or acceptable and who usually opposes changes to traditional methods and practices

shootout: a competition that is used to decide the winner at the end of a tie game by giving each team a particular number of chances to shoot the ball or puck into the goal

concussions: an injury to the brain that is caused by something hitting the head very hard

CHAPTER 8

THE FUTURE OF ICE HOCKEY

Sports adapt and change to reflect the society that supports and sustains them, and hockey is no different. Sensitivity and more of a common-sense approach to violence have had a significant impact on the sport, and that will continue to evolve. The audience desire for offense appears to be insatiable, and the NHL continues to try and feed it. The new generation of players will play in a league that is not exactly the same as the one they grew up watching.

NEW RULES

There was a time in the NHL when it was OK for regular-season games to end in a tie. That time ended in 2005 with the introduction, after a five-minute four-on-four overtime period, of the shootout, which is a one-on-one skills competition between the puck carrier and the goaltender. That posed a new problem, however. Many **purists** complained that even though it may be a fan-friendly solution to eliminating ties, which is still desired, it was such a specialized element of the game that it didn't necessarily reflect who the better team was on that night.

Columbus Blue Jackets and Carolina Hurricanes.

NHL officials can now use instant replay to review goaltender interference and offsides on scoring plays

The **shootout** is necessary, however, to avoid games that stretch into the middle of the night during the season. To find a way to have fewer shootouts, the overtime period was changed to three-on-three for the 2015-2016 season. The idea is that the open ice will create more opportunities to end the game before a shootout would be necessary.

VIDEO GAMES

The ready availability of instant replay and multiple camera angles have made it easy for professional sports leagues to adopt technology to help make games as fair as possible. Some sports have embraced technology more readily than others. In hockey, standardized video replay to determine if goals have been scored was implemented in 2003. In 2015, the NHL expanded video review situations to include coach's challenges.

Head coaches will be able to challenge on-ice officials' calls in certain instances. All of them involve a goal being scored. The call can be challenged in these cases:

- a goal is scored on a play that may have been offside at the blue line
- a goal is scored or disallowed on a play where the goaltender may have been interfered with

A team must have a time-out remaining to make a challenge because they must forfeit a time-out if the original call is upheld. In the final minute of regulation and in overtime, the coach's challenge is eliminated, and the NHL initiates any and all reviews.

There have been rumors that the league also has considered embedding cameras in each goalpost to provide other close-up angles besides the one from the camera in the back center of the net.

Rangers goalie Steve Valiquette watches the puck go into his glove for a save in a game against the Flyers at the Wachovia Center January 31, 2008, in Philadelphia, PA.

The First Niagara Center, Buffalo Sabres

Madison Square Garden, New York Rangers

Tampa Bay Times Forum,
Tampa Bay Lightning

Honda Center, Anaheim Ducks

Pepsi Center, Colorado Avalanche

Scotiabank Saddledome, Calgary Flames

WOMEN IN HOCKEY

One of the fastest-growing segments of the game is women's hockey. The first Women's World Championship was held in 1990. Hockey was added as an Olympic sport at the 1998 Games in Nagano, Japan. In 1990, USA Hockey had just over 6,000 registered players. In 2012, that number was more than 65,000. In both Canada and the United States, about 12 percent of all registered players are female, and that number is expected to rise.

The United States won the inaugural women's Olympic tournament in 1998, but Canada has won the gold every time since. Either the United States or Canada has won every one of the 16 International Ice Hockey Federation World Championships. In fact, the two countries have played each other in every gold medal game. In the future, that may soon change. Women's hockey is improving in traditional hockey-playing countries like Sweden, Finland, and Russia. It might not be long before they are challenging the North American teams for international gold.

Canada vs. USA ice hockey Women's Gold Medal Ceremony at the Sochi 2014 Olympic Games

CONCUSSIONS AND FIGHTING

Collisions and fistfights have been a part of hockey since its inception. The collisions are a by-product of the game. The fistfights, on the other hand, are tolerated but have been significantly reduced in recent years. With an emphasis on speed and skill, fewer and fewer roster spots are available for players who can contribute little other than fighting. In the 2014–2015 season, there were just over 400 fighting majors. In 2008–2009, there were 734. The role of fighting in the game is shrinking and will likely continue to do so in the future.

A fight breaks out at an AHL game between the Toronto Marlies and Hamilton Bulldogs.

Fighting rules now make it illegal for players to remove their helmets during a fight. This is just one of several rules the NHL has enacted since 2010 to reduce the number of **concussions** suffered by players. Checks that primarily contact the head are also illegal, as the NHL looks to a future when players aren't faced with long-term effects of post-concussion syndrome or with losing star players like Sidney Crosby, who missed major parts of the 2010–2011 and 2011–2012 seasons with concussions.

HOCKEY IS FOR EVERYONE

Willie O'Ree was the first player of black descent in the NHL, debuting with Boston in 1958. After he retired in 1979, O'Ree worked with the NHL to grow the game in minority communities. As part of the NHL's diversity initiative, the Hockey Is for Everyone youth development program helps youth hockey programs across North America that have predominantly minority enrollment and promotes its mission to offer kids from all backgrounds the opportunity to play the sport. The league kicks in money, and many players give their time to support the initiative. With young, up-and-coming black players like Seth Jones, Darnell Nurse, Malcolm Subban, and Anthony Duclair poised to be the next stars of the league, positive examples are coming of what diversity will bring for the future.

*Buffalo Sabre Nathan Gerbe battles with
Carolina Hurricane Bobby Sanguinetti during an NHL game.*

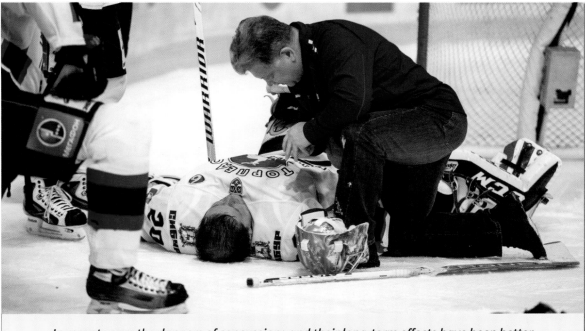

*In recent years the dangers of concussions and their long-term effects have been better
understood, and rules are now in place to reduce the occurrence of head injuries.*

FUTURE STARS

Connor McDavid is set to be the face of the NHL through 2035 and beyond. The first overall pick in the 2015 NHL draft, he is expected to be a generational talent along the lines of Sidney Crosby and Alexander Ovechkin. In the 2014–2015 season with the Erie Otters of the Major Junior Ontario Hockey League (OHL), McDavid scored 44 goals and 76 assists for 120 points in 47 games. That's an astounding 2.5 points per game. In the OHL playoffs, he scored 49 points in 20 games. The Edmonton Oilers expect him to be the face of their franchise for decades to come.

Auston Matthews is a year younger than McDavid. The projected first overall pick in the 2016 draft is also expected to be a generational talent. Not since Ovechkin and Crosby were selected in back-to-back years in 2004 and 2005 have two such talents hit the league so close together. Matthews was raised in Arizona, which is a very rare place for a top prospect to grow up. Playing with the U.S. Development Team, he scored 116 points in 60 games in 2014–2015.

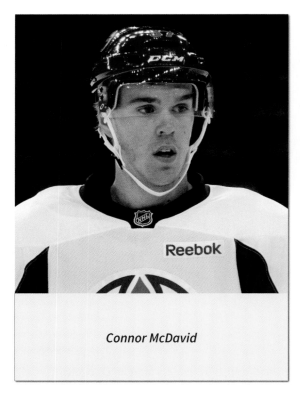

Connor McDavid

Future NHL stars like Auston Matthews join the league through the Entry Draft, where teams take turns selecting teenaged prospects.

Text-Dependent Questions:

1. In what year did the NHL expand video review situations to include coach's challenges?

2. What is one of the fastest-growing segments of the game?

3. Name two up-and-coming stars.

Research Project:

Write about how you think the sport of hockey will change in the future.

GLOSSARY OF HOCKEY TERMS

assist: passing to a teammate who scores a goal, also including unintentional deflections. For each goal, there can be up to two assists.

blue lines: at 60 feet (18.3 m) from each goal, the blue lines are as wide as the ice.

center: the player on the forward line who has a winger on either side. Coaches often play the most skilled offensive player as center.

check: sliding into an opponent to knock him or her off balance and out of the play.

defensemen: players who try to minimize scoring attempts. Defensemen usually play in set pairs.

face-off: when an official drops the puck between two players, who each try to get the puck to his or her own team. This is how play begins at the start of a period or after a penalty call.

five-hole: one of the places in the goal that players aim to score, specifically between a goaltender's legs—a popular spot because sometimes the goalie can't close his or her legs fast enough. Other areas are the upper left, upper right, lower left, and lower right corners of the goal.

forwards: the players on offense—centers and wingers. Some forwards also have great defensive abilities against the opposing team's most skilled attackers. Forwards usually work as a set unit of three players.

goal: a score, when the puck completely crosses the goal line, an imaginary plane rising above the goal line and between the posts and the crossbar. Goal judges and instant replay are used to confirm goals.

goal line: the narrow red line used to determine goals and icing calls. It runs from board to board across the ice near the end of the rink.

icing: when a player behind the red line hits the puck the length of the ice, and the first person to touch the puck is a defender other than the goaltender. When icing is called, there is a face-off in the defensive zone of the team that iced the puck.

line change: switching players during a stoppage in play or during the game. Line changes help teams keep players fresh and able to keep up with the speed of the game.

linesmen: the two officials who watch for offsides and icing calls. They usually stay near the blue lines.

offsides: when an offensive player crosses the attacking blue line before the puck. Officials stop play and start a face-off outside the zone.

one-timer: a shot or pass in which the player redirects the puck with his or her stick without first controlling it. One-timers give players a quick release, leaving the goalie little time to react.

overtime: the period that occurs after a game ends in a tie. In the regular season, teams play just one 5-minute overtime whether or not another goal is scored. In the playoffs, teams play 20-minute overtime periods until a goal is scored.

penalties: infractions (boarding, charging, holding, cross-checking, roughing, and more) that result in offenders staying in the penalty box, usually for two minutes. Major penalties can mean four minutes.

penalty shot: awarded when a defender commits a penalty against an attacker with a clear breakaway. The offensive play takes a one-on-one shot against the goaltender.

point: 1) assists plus goals for individual players.
2) during the regular season, teams earn two points for a win, one for a tie or overtime loss, and nothing for a loss in regulation.

power play: when one team plays with more players because of penalties. Most power plays are five-on-four, not counting the goalies. After minor penalties, power plays end if the advantaged team scores a goal.

plus/minus: unique to hockey, this statistic describes an individual player's offensive and defensive value. Every goal scored for his or her team when the player is on the ice (power play goals excepted) counts as a point, and similarly, a point is subtracted for every goal scored against.

puck: a flat rubber disk used to play the game of hockey.

red line: center ice, the 1-foot-wide (30.5 cm) line that runs the width of the ice from side to side and divides the ice into halves.

referees: game officials who call penalties and manage the action. The NHL uses two referees per game.

save: when a goaltender prevents a goal by catching the puck or stopping or deflecting it.

shift: a player's turn on the ice, usually about 90 seconds long, before a line change.

shorthanded: when a team has fewer players on the ice than the opposing team during a power play. If a team with fewer players scores, it is called a shorthanded goal.

slap shot: when a player draws back the stick well off the ice to strike the puck hard at the goal. The fastest shots are often more than 90 miles per hour (144.8 km/h).

tie: when the score is equal after regulation and 5 minutes of overtime. To track team statistics, both teams receive one point.

wingers: the two forwards that play along each side of the center—right and left.

wrist shot: a shot, very useful near the goal, in which the player does not lift the stick to strike the puck. The player uses his or her hands only.

Zamboni: a large, tractor-like machine, used before games and between periods, that scrapes off chipped ice and lays down a thin layer of water that immediately freezes smooth to provide a better, safer playing surface.

CHRONOLOGY

1893 Lord Stanley buys and donates a silver punch bowl—the Stanley Cup—for $48.67 to be used for hockey competition.

1917 National Hockey League (NHL) is organized November 22 in Montréal. Montréal Wanderers, Montréal Canadiens, Ottawa Senators, Quebec Bulldogs, and Toronto Arenas join the new league, but Quebec does not start until 1919.

1967–68 Six new teams join the NHL: California Seals, Los Angeles Kings, Minnesota North Stars, Philadelphia Flyers, Pittsburgh Penguins, and St. Louis Blues. New teams play in the West Division while the remaining six teams play in the East Division.

1972 NHL star Bobby Hull signs for a record $2.75 million in salary and bonuses with the Winnipeg Jets, jumping to the new World Hockey Association (WHA).

1979 The WHA and NHL merge, with the NHL keeping four WHA teams: the Hartford Whalers, Quebec Nordiques, Winnipeg Jets, and Edmonton Oilers.

1991 Video review is implemented in situations where it is unclear if a goal has been scored or not.

1992–1993 Ottawa Senators and Tampa Bay Lightning added, making the NHL a 24-team league.

1993–1994 The NHL adds the Mighty Ducks of Anaheim and Florida Panthers, increasing the league to 26 teams. A Minnesota franchise shifts to Dallas and is named the Dallas Stars.

1994–1995 Labor disruption forces cancelation of 468 games from October 1, 1994, to January 19, 1995. Clubs play a 48-game schedule.

1995–1996 Quebec franchise transfers to Denver as the Colorado Avalanche. In the first season in Colorado, the Avalanche wins the 1996 Stanley Cup.

1996–1997 Winnipeg franchise transfers to Phoenix as the Phoenix Coyotes. The Hartford franchise moves to Carolina as the Carolina Hurricanes.

1998 The NHL goes from one on-ice referee to two. The Nashville Predators enter the NHL.

1999 The Atlanta Thrashers come on board.

2000 The Minnesota Wild and Columbus Blue Jackets begin play.

2002 NHL players compete in the Olympic Games Ice Hockey Tournament.

2004–2005 The entire season is lost due to a labor dispute. For only the second time in history, the Stanley Cup is not awarded.

2005 The shootout is implemented to break ties in games that have not been decided in an overtime period.

2007 Sidney Crosby of Pittsburgh wins the scoring title at 19, the youngest Art Ross Trophy winner in history.

2011 The NHL introduces new rules designed to reduce the number of player concussions, along with new protocols to help diagnose concussions more quickly. The Atlanta franchise moves to Winnipeg, and the Jets are reborn.

2015 The NHL introduces three-on-three play in overtime to reduce the number of shootouts.

Hockey Today: In 2016, the New Jersey Devils retired the jersey of three-time Stanley Cup champion goalie Martin Brodeur. Brodeur will be eligible for the Hall of Fame in 2018, and will surely be a first ballot inductee. Other possible inductees that year could include Mark Recchi, Dave Andreychuk, Paul Kariya and Keith Tkachuk.

FURTHER READING:

Cameron, Steve. *Hockey Hall of Fame Book of Players.* Firefly Books, 2013

Sports Illustrated. *The Hockey Book.* Sports Illustrated, 2010

Duhatschek, Eric, and Tremblay, Rejean. *One Hundred Years of Hockey.* Thunder Bay Press, 1999

Podnieks, Andrew. *Lord Stanley's Cup.* Triumph Books, 2004

INTERNET RESOURCES:

National Hockey League http://www.nhl.com/

International Ice Hockey Federation http://www.iihf.com/

Hockey Hall of Fame https://www.hhof.com/

The Hockey News http://www.thehockeynews.com/

VIDEO CREDITS:

The Great Comeback (pg 8) https://www.youtube.com/watch?v=cnO1QWbUjhU

Five Straight Cups (pg 9) https://www.youtube.com/watch?v=kUjYYB0A4R0

Orr Takes Flight (pg 10) http://video.nhl.com/videocenter/console?id=465466

"Henderson Has Scored for Canada" (pg 11) https://www.youtube.com/watch?v=lMf2fAXPS1Q

The Miracle on Ice (pg 12) https://www.youtube.com/watch?v=qYscemhnf88

The Guarantee (pg 13) http://video.rangers.nhl.com/videocenter/console?id=115487

Bourque Gets His Cup (pg 14) http://video.avalanche.nhl.com/videocenter/console?id=250535

Crosby Is Golden (pg 15) http://video.nhl.com/videocenter/console?id=556709

QR CODES AND LINKS TO THIRD-PARTY CONTENT

You may gain access to certain third-party content ("Third-Party Sites") by scanning and using the QR Codes that appear in this publication (the "QR Codes"). We do not operate or control in any respect any information, products, or services on such Third-Party Sites linked to by us via the QR Codes included in this publication, and we assume no responsibility for any materials you may access using the QR Codes. Your use of the QR Codes may be subject to terms, limitations, or restrictions set forth in the applicable terms of use or otherwise established by the owners of the Third-Party Sites. Our linking to such Third-Party Sites via the QR Codes does not imply an endorsement or sponsorship of such Third-Party Sites, or the information, products, or services offered on or through the Third- Party Sites, nor does it imply an endorsement or sponsorship of this publication by the owners of such Third-Party Sites.

PICTURE CREDITS

INDEX

In this index, page numbers in **bold italics** font indicate photos or videos.

INDEX